W9-BXE-798

First Facts®

MY FIRST GUIDE TO
ROBOTS

by Kathryn Clay

CAPSTONE PRESS
a capstone imprint

First Facts are published by Capstone Press,
1710 Roe Crest Drive, North Mankato, Minnesota 56003
www.capstonepub.com

Library of Congress Cataloging-in-Publication Data
Clay, Kathryn, author.
  My first guide to robots / by Kathryn Clay.
      pages cm.—(First facts. My first guides)
  Includes bibliographical references and index.
  Summary: "Simple text and large, colorful photographs introduce young readers to robots"—Provided by publisher.
  Audience: K–3.
  ISBN 978-1-4914-2049-2 (library binding)
  ISBN 978-1-4914-2255-7 (ebook PDF)
1. Robots—Juvenile literature. I. Title.
  TJ211.2.C5387 2015
  629.8'92—dc23   2014032621

Editorial Credits
Alesha Sullivan, editor; Tracy McCabe, designer; Jo Miller, media researcher; Katy LaVigne, production specialist

Photo Credits
Alamy: PV Collection, 9 (both), Xinhua, 21 (bottom); NASA, 13, 15; NASA: JPL-Caltech, cover; Newscom: EPA/Salvatore di Nolfi, 11 (bottom), Feature Photo Service, 21(top), Getty Images/AFP/Toshifumi Kitamura, 17, Reuters/Francois Lenoir, 19, Reuters/Kim Kyung-Hoon, 11 (top); Shutterstock/rezachka, 5; Superstock: Science Faction/Ed Darack, cover (top left); Wikimedia: Photo by Erik Möller. Leonardo da Vinci. Mensch/Erfinder/Genie exhibit, Berlin 2005, 7

Design Elements
Shutterstock: ayelet-keshet, ExpressVectors, Merydolla

Printed in the United States of America in North Mankato, Minnesota.
092014   008482CGS15

TABLE OF CONTENTS

ROBOTS ALL AROUND

Do you have a difficult or boring task? Send in a robot! For years people imagined machines that worked like people. Now hardworking robots are found all around us. Robots in factories carry heavy loads. Some doctors use robots when performing operations. Robots are made to play games against each other.

robots in a factory

ROBOT HISTORY

Until 1920 no one had ever used the term "robot." Then Karel Capek wrote about machines that acted like humans. He called them *robota*, which means "worker" in the Czech language.

FACT

People were thinking about humanlike machines long before Capek wrote about them. Italian artist Leonardo da Vinci was drawing robot knights in the 1400s. In 1774 Pierre Jaquet-Droz made a small figure that could write words on paper.

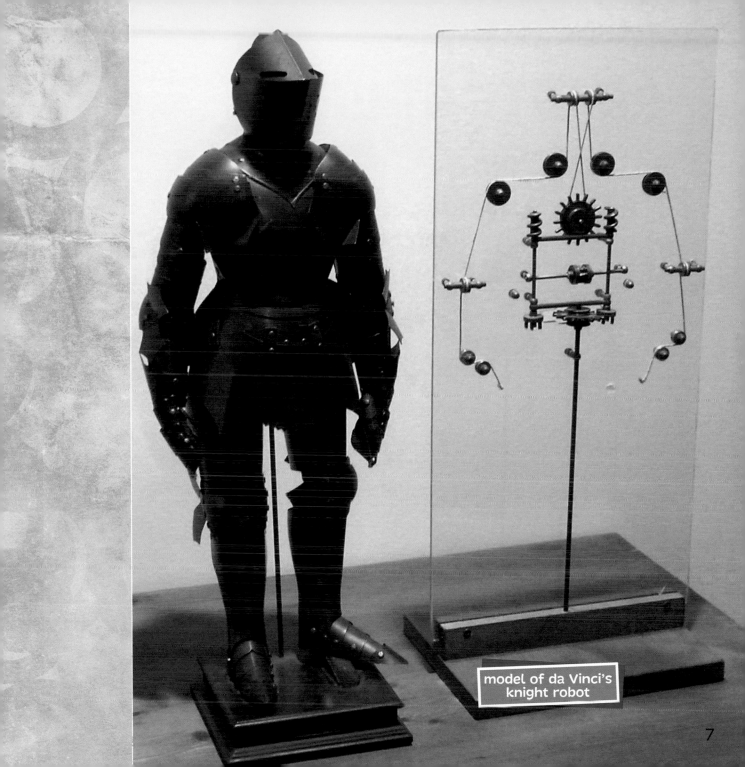

model of da Vinci's knight robot

ROBOTS AT WORK

Factories began using robots in the 1960s. Unimate was a big robotic arm. The robot stacked metal plates in a car factory. Today factory robots can do many more advanced jobs. Some robots use tiny "fingers" to tighten bolts and fix computer parts.

Robots are not limited to factory work. Robots on farms can feed and milk cows. AgAnts are small robots that work in fields. Groups of AgAnts swarm together to pull out weeds.

Unimate's long arm

Unimate in a factory

Paro is a robotic harp seal that acts like a real pet. Since 2003 these mechanical animals have appeared in hospitals and nursing homes. Paro recognizes its own name and sounds like a real baby seal.

Some **surgeons** use robots for difficult operations. More than 1.5 million surgeries have used the da Vinci Surgical System. Its robotic arms make small movements in a patient's body.

FACT

A robot named Smart Restaurant chops onions and tomatoes. Then it helps build up to 360 burgers per hour.

Paro

da Vinci surgical system

surgeon—a doctor who performs operations

ROBOT SPACE EXPLORERS

Robots in outer space help **astronauts** to gather information. Canadarm 2's long robotic arm moves objects outside of a spacecraft where astronauts live. **Orbiters** and **rovers** study the surface of other planets. Rovers' robot arms scrape rock samples to send back to Earth.

astronaut—a person who is trained to live and work in space
orbiter—a spacecraft that orbits a planet or other space objects
rover—a small remote control vehicle used to explore objects in space

Canadarm 2 on the International Space Station

FACT

The Cassini orbiter reached Saturn in 2004. That same year rovers Opportunity and Spirit landed on Mars. Opportunity still studies the planet today.

UNDERWATER ROBOT EXPLORERS

Robots are also used to explore the deepest parts of the ocean. Experts use cameras to steer Remotely Operated Vehicles (ROVs). ROVs explore sunken ships and fix oil rig machines in deep ocean waters.

Autonomous Underwater Vehicles (AUVs) control themselves. Some AUVs run on **solar power**. Scientists use AUVs to study the ocean floor.

FACT
The Bluefin-12D AUV runs up to 30 hours before its battery needs to be recharged.

underwater ROV

autonomous—able to control oneself; autonomous robots are not operated by remote control

solar power—energy produced by the sun

ROBOTS TO THE RESCUE

Search and rescue robots help after disasters. Urbie's strong **treads** move the robot over rough ground.

At 11.5 feet (3.5 meters), Enryu frees people trapped in rubble. Its strong arms can lift cars out of the way.

PackBot robots are small enough to fit inside of a backpack. Soldiers use a type of PackBot to check for hidden bombs. TALON robots use cameras to **disarm** bombs from a distance.

Enryu

tmsuk

北九州市消防局　独立行政法人 消防研究所

treads—the ridges on a tire that help the tire grip the road or ground

disarm—to make a bomb stop working

HUMANOIDS

Some robots look more like people than machines. These humanoids can walk, talk, sing, and dance.

In 2007 Repilee Q1Expo was one of the most lifelike robots in the world. The robot had artificial "skin." It blinked and even appeared to breathe.

The Honda Company introduced ASIMO in 2000. By 2012 ASIMO could run and climb stairs.

humanoid—a robot that has a human form
artificial—not real

ASIMO

ROBOT COMPETITIONS

Some builders make robots designed to fight. Robot fighters push each other into sharp floor spikes and spinning saws. The robots fight for a set number of minutes or until a robot can no longer move.

Humanoid robots compete in the Robocup soccer tournament. They can run and kick like humans. Each year the RoboGames include more than 50 robot competitions. Robots wrestle, lift weights, and even play the piano.

robot fighters

humanoids

Glossary

artificial (ar-tih-FISH-uhl)—not real

astronaut (AS-truh-nawt)—a person who is trained to live and work in space

autonomous (aw-TAH-nuh-muhss)—able to control oneself; autonomous robots are not operated by remote control

disarm (dis-AHRM)—to make a bomb stop working

humanoid (HYOO-muh-noyd)—a robot that has a human form

International Space Station (in-tur-NASH-uh-nuhl SPAYSS STAY-shuhn)—a place for astronauts to live and work in space

orbiter (OR-bit-ur)—a spacecraft that orbits a planet or other space objects

rover (ROH-vur)— a small remote control vehicle used to explore objects in space

solar power (SOH-lur POU-ur)—energy produced by the sun

surgeon (SUR-juhn)—a doctor who performs operations

treads (TREDS)—the ridges on a tire that help the tire grip the road or ground

Read More

Alpert, Barbara. *U.S. Military Robots*. U.S. Military Technology. North Mankato, Minn.: Capstone Press, 2013.

Oxlade, Chris. *Robots*. Explorers. New York: Kingfisher, 2013.

Stewart, Melissa. *Robots*. National Geographic Readers. Washington, D.C.: National Geographic, 2014.

Internet Sites

FactHound offers a safe, fun way to find Internet sites related to this book. All of the sites on FactHound have been researched by our staff.

Here's all you do:

Visit *www.facthound.com*

Type in this code: 9781491420492

Check out projects, games and lots more at
www.capstonekids.com

Critical Thinking Using the Common Core

1. What do underwater robots do? (Key Ideas and Details)

2. Think about a job you would like to have. How would you use robots to help you do your job? (Integration of Knowledge and Ideas)

Index